An Order of Marriage

AN ORDER OF MARRIAGE

For Christians
from Different Churches

The Joint Liturgical Group
of Great Britain

CANTERBURY
PRESS
Norwich

© The Joint Liturgical Group of Great Britain, 1999

First published in 1999 by
The Canterbury Press Norwich
(a publishing imprint of Hymns Ancient & Modern
Limited, a registered charity)
St Mary's Works, St Mary's Plain
Norwich, Norfolk, NR3 3BH.

British Library Cataloguing in Publication Data.

A catalogue record for this book is available
from the British Library.

ISBN 1-85311-309-3

Typeset by Rowland Phototypesetting Ltd,
Bury St Edmunds, Suffolk.
Printed and bound in Great Britain by
Redwood Books
Trowbridge, Wiltshire.

CONTENTS

INTRODUCTION

When a man and woman from different churches fall in love and wish to marry, they present the Church of Christ at the same time with a sign of Christ's love for his Church and with a painful reminder of the divisions that mar our experience of the Church. Although the degree of commitment of the two people to their respective traditions may vary, they will bring to their marriage this experience of a divided Church. While the possibility exists that they will find their marriage richly supported by both traditions, there is equally a danger that division within the body of Christ will invade and undermine their marriage. At York, during his visit to these islands in 1982, Pope John Paul II addressed such couples in these words, 'You live in your marriage the hopes and difficulties of the path to Christian unity.'

In 1994, Churches Together in England and CYTUN (Churches Together in Wales) published *Churches Together in Marriage: Pastoral Care of Interchurch Families*. In the course of a thorough discussion of issues raised by interchurch marriages, the report identifies a number of Guidelines and Recommendations which we reproduce in Appendix 1. Its Foreword says,

> Interchurch marriages and their families constitute a challenge to the churches since they cut across our well established lines of division. They challenge the churches to provide ecumenical possibilities of joint preparation for interchurch marriages, greater ecumenical participation in the celebration of the wedding ceremonies and joint pastoral care of interchurch families throughout life.

With this order of service the Joint Liturgical Group seeks to contribute to the recognition and support of such couples. Since 1963, the Joint Liturgical Group has sought to serve the churches in Britain in the quest for common understandings of and texts for worship. Arising from consultations in 1989 it accepted the task of framing a marriage service which might be offered to the churches for the celebration of such marriages.

The Joint Liturgical Group includes representatives appointed by various churches in the United Kingdom. Its membership over the period in which this rite has been prepared has included people who have been closely involved in revising the marriage rites of various churches as well as one person who helped draft *A Celebration of Christian Marriage: An Ecumenical Liturgy* (1985) produced by the Consultation of Common Texts (CCT) in North America. We have consulted beyond our membership and have been grateful for formal and informal contacts with couples involved in interchurch marriages. We are grateful to Ruth Reardon, Secretary of the Association of Interchurch Families, for her attendance, encouragement and advice. We were grateful to the Pastoral Liturgy Committee of the Roman Catholic Bishops' Conference for England and Wales for making available to us the draft *Order of Christian Marriage* which has now been submitted to Rome for confirmation.

In producing this service we have been aware of the common roots that British marriage rites have in the usage of Sarum as well as of fresh thinking about the liturgical form of marriage. Although we welcome attempts to provide additional liturgical rites to help couple and community establish a marriage, we decided that the interests of interchurch couples would be best served by a single main rite with, as far as possible, a fixed structure. The order that we have produced seeks to give a balanced place to different parts of the tradition of marriage: the Western emphasis on consent in which a couple's promise is recognized and supported; the Jewish and Eastern emphasis that sees the marriage as a gift to be welcomed in blessing by couple and community; the civic tradition that requires the public registration and recognition of the marriage.

The established tradition of the Joint Liturgical Group has been to seek to be guided by the best liturgical thinking and then to offer

8

its work to the churches for them to use or adapt as they think fit. Forms of service produced by the Joint Liturgical Group have usually been prefaced by the following explanation.

It is clearly to be understood that any work produced by this Group will have no authority greater than that which its own members give to it by their own weight; but it will be for particular Churches, through their own customary modes of decision, to make use of the results if they are willing to do so.

The complexities both of state law and of the procedures for regulating and authorizing liturgies in the different churches will inevitably involve minor adjustments to the rite that we offer here. The rite set out in this booklet is designed to meet the current legal requirements for religious marriages in England and Wales (except for the Church of England and the Church in Wales for whom the law makes separate provision). Account has been taken of the Marriage Ceremony (Prescribed Words) Act 1996. A different, and more flexible, system operates in Scotland. Appendix 2 gives some indication of the processes that will need to be adopted for this rite to be used in different churches. Clearly if changes go substantially beyond those necessary to meet legal requirements something of the ecumenical character of this rite will be lost.

Charles Robertson,
Chairman,
The Joint Liturgical Group of Great Britain

OUTLINE OF THE RITE

An asterisk (*) indicates optional elements that may be included where appropriate.

Hymns may be introduced at any appropriate point.

PREPARATION AND INTRODUCTION

Welcome
Greeting
Opening Prayer
Statement of Marriage
Legal Declarations
Declaration of Intent
*Affirmation by Families and Congregation
Prayer of Invocation

MINISTRY OF THE WORD

Readings from Scripture
Sermon
Hymn

THE MARRIAGE

Prayer for Grace
The Marriage Vows (Exchange of Consent)
The Giving of the Ring(s)
The Prayer of Blessing
The Announcement of Marriage
[The Prayer of Blessing – alternative position]
*Presentation of Gift(s) from the Churches
Signing of Registers
Hymn

AFTER THE MARRIAGE

Prayers
The Lord's Prayer
*The Peace
*Holy Communion
Dismissal of the Congregation
[Signing of Registers – alternative position]

NOTES

1. Where a couple come to be married who belong to different
   churches they should be welcomed with warmth and
   understanding. Preparation for marriage and the planning of the
   wedding should be conducted with respect for their individual
   circumstances. The report *Churches Together in Marriage* (1994)
   may be used as a guide in identifying and avoiding pitfalls in the
   pastoral care of such couples. (The Guidelines and Recommendations from this report can be found in Appendix 1.)

11

2. It is desirable that clergy from the denominations or traditions represented by the couple take leading roles in the service. The couple and clergy should meet to plan the service together.

3. The following order is set out so as to enable ministers from both churches to participate. The Exchange of Marriage Vows (section 16) and the Announcement of Marriage (section 20) must be led by the minister authorized to officiate at the marriage, who should also participate in the Prayer of Blessing (section 19).

4. Sensitive adaptation of some of the prayers may be required. Parts indicated for different voices may be said by parents, relatives, or friends. Where prayers are printed as for a single voice, they may be adapted so that more than one voice may be used.

5. In the Legal Declarations (section 7) and the Exchange of Marriage Vows (section 16) the words currently required by law for Roman Catholic and Free Church marriages in England and Wales are printed in capital letters. For these churches the law requires that they must take place in the presence of the Authorized Person (or the Registrar) and two witnesses. At these points the full names of the parties must be used.

6. In cases where prayers for the birth of children are not appropriate they may be omitted.

7. It may be helpful to print the version of the Lord's Prayer to be used, so that the whole congregation can say the same version of the prayer together.

8. The use of symbols during the service is to be encouraged. For example, two candles may be lit early in the service to represent the two people who are to be married and their two families; later a third candle is lit to represent the new relationship celebrated in the marriage.

ORDER FOR THE MARRIAGE OF CHRISTIANS FROM DIFFERENT CHURCHES

PREPARATION AND INTRODUCTION

1. WELCOME

The minister(s) informally welcome(s) the bride or couple at the church door.

The wedding party processes into the church.

2. GREETING

The people are greeted and called to worship.

> The grace of our lord Jesus Christ, the love of God,
> and the fellowship of the Holy Spirit be with you all.

and

> God is love, and those who live in love live in God,
> and God lives in them.

13

3. *A hymn of praise may be sung.*

4. OPENING PRAYER

Either

Almighty God,
to whom all hearts are open,
all desires known,
and from whom no secrets are hidden:
cleanse the thoughts of our hearts
by the inspiration of your Holy Spirit,
that we may perfectly love you,
and worthily magnify your holy name;
through Christ our Lord. Amen.

or

Eternal God,
you are with us
in the fulness of your love:

love made flesh for us,
bearing the weight of human guilt and shame;
love which fills our hearts
and binds us to each other,
creating communion from separation;
love which you are willing to renew continually
in the lives of *N* and *N*.

Make them a sign to us
of your love in all creation;
of your forgiveness and self-sacrifice
that give us hope;
and of our being together, with you,
for lasting delight
and indestructible peace.

14

By your Holy Spirit,
reveal your glory through us all,
and let the world receive in us
the healing and joy of Christ,
as you keep us in eternal life. Amen.

5. *A hymn of praise may be sung.*

6. STATEMENT OF MARRIAGE

Either

We have come together in the presence of God,
to witness the wedding of *N* and *N*,
to rejoice with them
and to surround them with our prayers.
Marriage is a gift of God within creation.
We are created male and female in the image of God,
and in the life-long union of marriage
   we can know God's presence and grace.
As a man and woman give themselves to each other in love,
they are joined together as Christ is joined with the Church.
God has given us marriage
   so that husband and wife may live faithfully together.
In plenty or need, in joy or sorrow,
they give each other strength, friendship and healing.
With delight and tenderness they know each other in love,
and so belong to one another in honour and in joy.
In marriage, children may be born and nurtured
that they may grow up in the security of love
and come to experience the freedom of faith.
In marriage, husband and wife
   begin a new life together in the world.

15

They are a sign of unity and loyalty in a broken world
   and for a divided Church;
their covenanted love enriches society
   and strengthens community.
Marriage is a way of life made holy by God.
It is both joy and demand, grace and work.
It is a gift and calling of God
and is not to be entered into lightly or thoughtlessly,
but reverently and responsibly.
This is the way of life that *N* and *N* are now to begin.
They come to accept each other freely,
to give their consent to one another in solemn promises,
and to ask for God's blessing.

or

Minister 1: We have come together in the presence of God,
    to witness the wedding of *N* and *N*,
    to rejoice with them
    and to surround them with our prayers.

Minister 2: Marriage is a gift of God within creation.
    We are created male and female in the image of God,
    and in the life-long union of marriage
    we can know God's presence and grace.

Minister 1: As a man and a woman give themselves
    to each other in love,
    they are joined together
    as Christ is joined with the Church

Minister 2: God has given us marriage
    so that husband and wife may live faithfully together.
    In plenty or need, in joy or sorrow,
    they give each other strength, friendship and healing.

Minister 1: With delight and tenderness
    they know each other in love,
    and so belong to each other in honour and in joy.

Minister 2: In marriage, children may be born and nurtured
that they may grow up in the security of love
and come to experience the freedom of faith.

Minister 1: In marriage, husband and wife
begin a new life together in the world.
They are a sign of unity and loyalty
in a broken world and for a divided Church;
their covenanted love enriches society
and strengthens community.

Minister 2: Marriage is a way of life made holy by God.
It is both joy and demand, grace and work.

Minister 1: It is a gift and calling of God
and is not to be entered into lightly or thoughtlessly,
but reverently and responsibly.

Minister 2: This is the way of life that *N* and *N* are now to begin.
They come to accept each other freely,
to give their consent to one another in solemn
     promises,
and to ask for God's blessing.

7. LEGAL DECLARATIONS*

The minister says to the people:

N and *N* are now to make the declarations which the law requires.

The minister says to the man:

ARE YOU, *N*, FREE LAWFULLY TO MARRY *N*?

*See Note 5, p. 12.

17

The man says:

I AM.

The minister says to the woman:

ARE YOU, *N*, FREE LAWFULLY TO MARRY *N*?

The woman says:

I AM.

8. DECLARATION OF INTENT

A minister addresses the man:

N, will you take *N* to be your wife:
will you love her, comfort her, honour and protect her,
and, forsaking all others, be faithful to her
as long as you both shall live?

The man says:

I WILL.

A minister addresses the woman:

N, will you take *N* to be your husband:
will you love him, comfort him, honour and protect him,
and, forsaking all others, be faithful to him
as long as you both shall live?

The woman says:

I WILL.

9. AFFIRMATION BY FAMILIES AND CONGREGATION

[to be used where appropriate]

A minister says to the families:

Will you, the families of *N* and *N*,
give your love and blessing to this new family?

Members of the families say:

We will.

A minister says to the congregation:

Will all of you, by God's grace, do everything you can
to uphold and care for *N* and *N* in their life together?

The congregation says:

We will.

10. PRAYER OF INVOCATION

A minister says:

Eternal God, our maker and redeemer,
as you once gladdened the wedding at Cana
by the presence of your Son,
so by his presence now bring your joy to this day.
May we drink deeply from your boundless love
and know in our hearts the delights of your Holy Spirit.

19

Let the love we celebrate today be a sign of your eternal
love, and as we honour the union of a man and a woman
draw us into unity with you;
through Christ our Lord. **Amen.**

MINISTRY OF THE WORD

11. READINGS FROM THE SCRIPTURE

*Two readings from the Scripture are read. (Where there is good
reason only one reading may be used.) A Psalm or hymn may be sung
between the two readings or between the readings and the sermon.*

Genesis 1:26-8, 31a ; *or* 2:18-25; *or* Song of Solomon 7:10-13; *or*
8:6-7; *or* Hosea 2:16-23; *or* Tobit 8:4-8.

Psalms: 45 *or* 67 *or* 127 *or* 128.

1 Corinthians 13:1-8a, 13; *or* Ephesians 3:14-21; *or* Colossians
3:12-17; *or* 1 John 4:7-13; *or* Mark 10:6-9; *or* John 2:1-11, 12.

12. *A Psalm or hymn may be sung.*

13. *A sermon is preached.*

14. *A hymn may be sung.*

THE MARRIAGE

The bride and bridegroom stand in the sight of the congregation.

15. PRAYER FOR GRACE

Either

Gracious God,
as you have brought *N* and *N* together in love,
enable them through the power of your Holy Spirit
to make and keep the solemn promises of marriage,
through Jesus Christ our Lord. **Amen.**

or

God of love, ever gracious and kind,
we pray for *N* and *N*
as they make the promises of marriage.
May they know you
as the God of mercy and new beginnings,
who forgives our failures and renews our hope.
May the grace of Christ
be poured into their wedding
for celebration and for joy;
God of love, ever present and faithful,
may *N* and *N* know that their marriage is your delight and will.
May the promises they make govern their life together
as your presence surrounds them,
and your Spirit strengthens and guides them:
through Jesus Christ our Lord. **Amen.**

16. THE MARRIAGE VOWS

[Exchange of consent]

The minister addresses the couple.

21

N and *N*
we have heard and pondered God's word,
and considered the meaning of marriage.
Now, in the presence of God and this congregation,
join your hands and declare your consent
to become husband and wife.

The couple turn to face each other and join their right hands.

The man says to the woman in the presence of the Authorized Person:

I, *N*, TAKE YOU, *N*,
TO BE MY WEDDED WIFE,
to have and to hold
from this day forward;
for better, for worse,
for richer, for poorer,
in sickness and in health,
to love and to cherish,
till death us do part,
according to God's holy will,
and this is my solemn vow.

The woman says to the man in the presence of the Authorized Person:

I, *N*, TAKE YOU, *N*,
TO BE MY WEDDED HUSBAND,
to have and to hold
from this day forward;
for better, for worse,
for richer, for poorer,
in sickness and in health,
to love and to cherish,
till death us do part,
according to God's holy will,
and this is my solemn vow.

17. THE GIVING OF THE RING(S)

A minister prays:

Bless, O God, the giving of these rings:
may those who wear them
live in love and faithfulness
all their days,
through Jesus Christ our Lord. **Amen.**

(The prayer may be adapted if only one ring is given.)

These words may be used at the exchange of rings:

I give you this ring as a sign of our marriage.
With my body I honour you,
all that I am I give to you,
and all that I have I share with you,
within the love of God,
Father, Son and Holy Spirit.

(If there is only one ring, the woman may respond: 'I receive this ring. . . .')

Along with the ring(s), gold and silver or other tokens of shared life may be exchanged between the man and the woman.

18. THE PRAYER OF BLESSING

The prayer of blessing may be said here or after section 20. Three forms are set out here; alternative forms are set out in the Appendix of Additional Texts (pp. 31–39).

The couple may kneel.

First Form

May the Lord bless you and keep you;
the Lord make his face to shine upon you
and be gracious to you;
the Lord lift up his countenance upon you
and give you peace. **Amen.**

Eternal God,
you create us out of love
and will that we should love one another.
Bless this man and this woman,
made in your image,
who today become a sign of your covenant love.
[As once the glory of Christ was made known at their baptism,
so now bless this marriage with fulfilment and joy.]
By your Holy Spirit, fill bride and bridegroom
with wisdom and hope
that they may delight in your gift of marriage
and enrich one another in love and faithfulness. **Amen.**

Second Form

Minister 1: Blessed are you, Lord our God,
God of love, Creator of all.
All: **Blessed be God for ever.**

Bridegroom: Blessed are you, Lord our God,
you make us in your image and likeness.
All: **Blessed be God for ever.**

Bride: Blessed are you, Lord our God,
you make man and woman to reflect your glory.
All: **Blessed be God for ever.**

Bridegroom: Blessed are you, Lord our God,
you make us for joy and promise us life.
All: **Blessed be God for ever.**

Bride:	Blessed are you, Lord our God,
	you create a people to know your love.
All:	**Blessed be God for ever.**

Voice A:	May *N* and *N* enjoy the blessing of your kingdom.
(or	Give them faith and joy in their marriage.
Minister 2:)	Blessed are you, Lord our God,
	you give joy to bride and groom.
All:	**Blessed be God for ever.**

Voice B:	May their love be fruitful
(or	and their home a place of peace.
Minister 1:)	Blessed are you, Lord our God,
	you make marriage a sign of your love.
All:	**Blessed be God for ever.**

Minister 2:	May they know the love of the Father,
	the life of the Son,
	and the joy of the Spirit.
	Blessed are you, Lord our God,
	Lover, Beloved, and Friend of Love.
All:	**Blessed be God for ever.**

THIRD FORM

| *Minister 1:* | My dear friends, let us ask God to pour out his |
| | blessing on *N* and *N*. |

All pray in silence for a short while.

Minister 2:	Father,
	we thank you for your constant
	and faithful love,
	a love beyond our understanding,
	a love which calls us to yourself.

Minister 1: In that love, you breathe life into all creation.
Out of love, you sent your Son to live among us.
With that love the Holy Spirit sustains
and makes rich our lives.

Minister 2: Your Son Jesus Christ showed the depth of that love
as he gave himself up to death for our salvation.
Rising from the dead, he gave his Spirit to the Church,
that family of faith where we know and share his life.

Minister 1: In your kindness, look gently upon *N* and *N*
and transform them with this Spirit of love and peace.
May their love be ever constant and faithful.
May it reflect the perfect love
you have for all your children.

Minister 2: [Let their love be the source of new life.
Bless them with children.]
Make their union a meeting with Christ,
a healing and forgiveness for each other
and a certain help and strength in times of trouble.

Minister 1: May their care and concern for each other
light a fire of love and charity
in the hearts of their family,
earn them the admiration of their neighbours,
and be an inspiration to all whom they meet.

Minister 2: Heap your blessings upon them.
Fill their home with happiness and peace.
Grant them joy and many years,
and bring them at the end to everlasting life with you.

Minister 1: We ask this Father, in the name of Jesus,
who lives and reigns in glory
with you and the Holy Spirit,
God for ever and ever.

All: **Amen.**

19. THE ANNOUNCEMENT OF MARRIAGE

The minister says:

N and N,
in the presence of God and of this congregation,
you have declared that you will live together
   in Christian marriage.
You have given your consent,
and made your promises
and so you have married each other before God.
Now you are husband and wife and we greet you.
Those whom God has joined together, let no one separate.

The congregation may joyfully acclaim the couple.

20. PRESENTATION OF GIFT(S) FROM THE CHURCHES

Symbolic gifts may be presented to the couple by representatives of the church communities from which the couple come. As the gifts are given, the affirmation, support and good wishes of the churches for the couple may be voiced.

For example, a Bible may be presented with these words:

Let the message of Christ, in all its richness, find a home with you:
teach each other and advise each other in all wisdom.

(Colossians 3:16)

or

...... church wishes you well, and offers you this ......
for a gift on your wedding day.

21. SIGNING OF REGISTERS

This may take place here or later. The registration should be made as simple as possible, preferably in the church or chapel and in the sight of the congregation.

AFTER THE MARRIAGE

22. *A hymn may be sung.*

23. PRAYERS

There follow further prayers for the couple and for their families as well as more general prayers of concern for the Church and the world. These may include prayers offered by the couple or by members of their families. They are most appropriately prayers prepared for the occasion. Some model prayers are provided in the Appendix of Additional Texts, pp. 31–9.

24. THE LORD'S PRAYER

Either

> **Our Father, who art in heaven,**
> **hallowed be thy name;**
> **thy kingdom come;**
> **thy will be done;**
> **on earth as it is in heaven.**
> **Give us this day our daily bread.**
> **And forgive us our trespasses,**
> **as we forgive those who trespass against us.**

And lead us not into temptation,
but deliver us from evil.
For thine is the kingdom,
the power and the glory,
for ever and ever. Amen.

or

Our Father in heaven,
hallowed be your name,
your kingdom come,
your will be done,
on earth as in heaven.
Give us today our daily bread.
Forgive us our sins
as we forgive those who sin against us.
Save us from the time of trial
and deliver us from evil.
For the kingdom, the power, and the glory are yours,
now and for ever. Amen.

25. *A hymn may be sung.*

26. *The Peace may be shared. This may be followed by the celebration of Holy Communion.*

27. DISMISSAL OF THE CONGREGATION

Either

We have witnessed the wedding of *N* and *N*.
Let us keep them in our prayers
and encourage them with our love,
as we go in peace to love and serve Christ.

The blessing of God, the Father, the Son and the Holy Spirit,
be with you always. **Amen.**

or

May the God who made us for one another,
who loves us with a faithful love,
and whose Spirit makes us passionate and strong,
bless you and embrace you,
now and forever. **Amen.**

29. SIGNING OF REGISTERS

(if not earlier)

*The registers should be signed at this point if they have not been signed
earlier.*

APPENDIX 1: ADDITIONAL TEXTS

PRAYERS OF BLESSING

(Alternatives for section 18)

To be said either by one minister or by two ministers, representing the traditions or church communities from which the couple come.

FOURTH FORM

Minister 1: My dear friends,
let us ask God for his continued blessings
upon *N* and *N*.

All pray in silence for a short while.

Minister 2: Father most holy,
creator of the world and all it contains,
you made man and woman in your image
and on their companionship
bestowed generous blessings.
Hear our prayers for your son and daughter,
who are joined together in marriage.

Minister 1: May the fullness of your blessings
descend upon *N*, this bride,
and upon *N*, this bridegroom.
May the power of your Holy Spirit
kindle in their hearts the fire of your love,
so that, expressing their delight in each other,
they may adorn the human family with children
and enrich the church with new members.

Minister 2: Let them praise you, Lord, in times of joy
and turn to you in their sorrows;
let them find your help in their strivings
and know your comfort when hardship strikes.
Let them offer you prayers in the holy assembly
and stand as witnesses to you before the world.
Let them live a long and happy life
and welcome them at last to your heavenly kingdom
together with their friends who surround them today.

Minister 1: We ask this through Jesus Christ our Lord.

All: **Amen.**

FIFTH FORM

Most gracious God,
we give you thanks for your tender love
  in sending Jesus Christ
to come among us,
to be born of a human mother,
and to make the way of the cross to be the way of life.
We thank you for consecrating the union of man and
  woman in his name.
By the power of your Holy Spirit,
pour out the abundance of your blessing
  upon this man and this woman.
Defend them from every enemy.
Lead them into all peace.
Let their love for each other be a seal upon their hearts,
a mantle about their shoulders,
and a crown upon their foreheads.
Bless them in their work and in their companionship,
in their sleeping and in their waking,
in their joys and in their sorrows,
in their life and in their death.

32

Finally, in your mercy, bring them to that table
where your saints feast for ever in your heavenly home;
through Jesus Christ our Lord,
who with you and the Holy Spirit lives and reigns,
one God, for ever and ever. **Amen.**

Minister: Blessed are you God the Father:
All: **You give joy to bridegroom and bride.**

Minister: Blessed are you, Lord Jesus Christ:
All: **You have brought new life to the world.**

Minister: Blessed are you, Holy Spirit of God:
All: **You bring us together in love.**

Minister: Blessed are you, Father, Son and Holy Spirit,
All: **One God to be praised for ever. Amen.**

SIXTH FORM

Minister: Marriage is a gift from God.
              It is a blessing to be honoured
                 and welcomed by all.

Bride: I am my beloved's and he is mine.

Bridegroom: Together we will walk in the way of love.

Bride: Love is strong as death,
              passion fierce as the grave.

Bridegroom: Many waters cannot quench love
              neither can floods drown it.

Bride: Blessed be God whose love cannot fail.

Bridegroom: Blessed be God who keeps his promise for ever.

Bride: May the love of God bless and protect us.

Bridegroom: May the presence of Christ guide and renew us.

Voice A: May each day bring you happiness
               and may your love bring joy to others.

Voice B: May your life together be fruitful
               and your home be a place of peace.

Voice C: May you find faith in adversity
               and all your ways be holy.

Voice D: May you be honoured by those around you
               and enjoy the love of friends.

Minister 1: May the blessing of God surround you
               and renew you in forgiveness and love.

Minister 2: May God give you joy and wisdom
               and make your love a sign of hope.

All: **May the love of God,**
               Father, Son and Holy Spirit,
               keep you in life for ever.
               Blessed be God
               who gives joy to bride and bridegroom.
               Blessed be God for ever. Amen.

SEVENTH FORM

Minister: Let us pray.
               At the wedding in Cana,
               the king of all grace was there in person.
               Let us ask him to bless this couple,
               as he blessed that celebration in Galilee.

Bride: Jesus, son of Mary,
have mercy on us.

All: **You are King of Kings
and God of all creation.**

Bridegroom: Be at the start of our way
and at the end of our living.

All: **You are King of Kings
and God of all creation.**

Bride: Be at the awakening of our life
and at the darkening of our day.

All: **You are King of Kings
and God of all creation.**

Bridegroom: Go before us and with us
to the end of our undertaking.

All: **You are King of Kings
and God of all creation.**

Bride: Make us holy
in our living and in our growing.

All: **You are King of Kings
and God of all creation.**

Bridegroom: Make us holy
in all we are and have.

All: **You are King of Kings
and God of all creation.**

Bride: Make us holy
in our loving and our believing.

All: **You are King of Kings**
               and God of all creation.

Bridegroom: Our loving and our believing
               each day are for you.

All: **You are King of Kings**
               and God of all creation.

Voice A: May you be blessed in prosperity,
               blessed in sons and daughters,
               blessed on land and sea.

Voice B: May you be blessed in your love,
               blessed in your faithfulness,
               blessed in the heavenly kingdom,
               blessed by day and night.

Voice C: May the goodness of the sea be yours,
               the goodness of the land be yours,
               the goodness of heaven be yours.

Voice D: May each day bring you happiness,
               and no day leave you worse;
               may you be honoured and respected,
               and have the love of each person you meet.

Minister 1: Crown *N* and *N* with your blessing;
               through them renew your creation,
               establish them in your reign of love.

Minister 2: Make their home a place of peace,
               their companionship a sign of unity,
               their love a blessing to all.

Minister 1: Bless them always with joy and wisdom,
               refresh them with forgiveness and hope,
               bring them at last to the glory of heaven.

36

Minister 2: Protect them with the power of the Father,
enrich them with the life of the Spirit,
keep them in the way of your love,
Jesus, son of Mary.

All: **You are King of Kings**
and God of all creation.

PRAYERS

(Alternatives to section 23)

Minister 1: Friends of Christ,
in the midst of our joy and celebration
let us pray to God for this broken world.

Minister 2: For the Church throughout the world,
for its unity and peace,
for understanding between separated traditions,
and for all who confess the name of Christ,
let us pray to God.

Silence

Minister 1: For the world and all its people,
that the peace of Christ will touch all nations
and lead them to harmony and compassion,
let us pray to God.

Silence

Minister 2: For the integrity and peace of all creation;
for the feeding of the hungry,
and the freedom of the oppressed,
let us pray to God.

Silence

Minister 1: For all who are in need, sorrow, or trouble,
for the sick, the lonely and the homeless,
that they will know the strength of Christ,
let us pray to God.

Silence

Minister 2: For our families, communities and churches,
for love and kindness
among us and between us,
let us pray to God.

Silence

Minister 1: For all married people,
that they may know God's love
in times of happiness and trouble,
let us pray to God.

Silence

Minister 2: For those who have lost their partner,
in death, separation or divorce,
that they find strength and comfort,
let us pray to God.

Silence

Minister 1: For all people,
that they may know love in community
and their worth as individuals,
let us pray to God.

Silence

Minister 2: Gracious God,
you have made us in your own image
and given us to one another.
Hear our prayers,
that unity may overcome division,
   and joy overwhelm sorrow.
We ask this through Jesus Christ our Lord.

All: **Amen.**

APPENDIX 2: GUIDELINES AND RECOMMENDATIONS

[From *Churches Together in Marriage: Pastoral Care of Interchurch Families*, published by Churches Together in England & CYTUN (Churches Together in Wales) 1994]

GUIDELINES

G1 Welcome and encourage interchurch couples who present themselves; do not regard them as disloyal for wanting to marry across Christian divisions, but see them as a positive resource in the context of growing unity between the churches.

G2 See interchurch marriages as an opportunity for exercising pastoral care in a way that will have long-term benefits for relationships between local church congregations.

G3 Welcome both partners into the life of your church so far as they wish to be involved, respecting the fact there may also be a loyalty to another congregation.

G4 Help interchurch couples to see their differences as a source of growth rather than unfortunate obstacles to unity.

G5 Encourage interchurch couples to explore how they can remain attached to their two traditions, rather than presenting them with a one-church option as the only hope of success for their marriage.

G6 Realizing that interchurch couples can be helped a great deal by meeting others in similar situations, inform couples of the existence of the Association of Interchurch Families and encourage them to make contact with it if they wish to do so.

G7 Help engaged interchurch couples to recognize how their church loyalties and pattern of churchgoing may relate to their natural need to maintain both closeness to each other and a certain separateness.

G8 Work closely with pastors of other churches in marriage preparation and support, both for interchurch couples and more generally.

G9 In preparing for the wedding, look at all the options within the disciplines of the churches and do everything possible to make both partners feel at home in the service.

G10 Assess with other churches the scope to increase lay involvement in marriage preparation.

G11 Whatever provision made by the churches concerned with regard to second marriages, recognize the pastoral and spiritual help that the couple together, or one of the partners, may be looking for.

G12 Do everything possible to support interchurch parents who want to share the riches of both traditions with their children and bring them up within the life of two church communities; respect any feeling of double belonging on the part of the children, who should not be required to make an exclusive choice.

G13 Enable those involved in marriage preparation and support to be aware of the current policies and guidelines of your own and other churches on interchurch marriage.

G14 Have details of all the legal and canonical requirements for marriage at hand for reference when needed.

RECOMMENDATIONS

R1 That pastoral policy towards interchurch families should be based on seeing them as a promise, not a threat, and on a desire to help them make a positive contribution to the growing together of the churches.

R2 That the churches explore together the extent to which the sense of dual commitment/double belonging experienced by some interchurch families can be recognized pastorally and given formal expression in church discipline and structures.

R3 That the churches look together at the 'double belonging' experienced by some interchurch children and address the ecclesiological questions which this raises.

R4 That the churches together produce catechetical material which emphasizes what they have in common, but also shows where there are remaining differences.

R5 That the churches build on what has already been done in their liturgical commissions (or equivalent) and continue to work for a common liturgy for the celebration of interchurch marriages which could be approved as appropriate.

R6 That local churches in appropriate groupings should be encouraged to explore opportunities for celebrating baptism together.

R7 That local churches in appropriate groupings should be encouraged to work together to establish opportunities for joint marriage preparation using suitably prepared teams including lay people.

R8 That local churches in appropriate groupings should be encouraged to work together to support families throughout the life cycle, wherever possible in co-operation with existing marriage and family agencies.

R9 That the churches at national level examine what machinery is needed to help them work together in marriage preparation and support, following up what has been done ecumenically to help the churches respond together to the International Year of the Family.

APPENDIX 3: THE USE OF THIS SERVICE IN DIFFERENT CHURCHES

This rite can be used by such churches as the Church of Scotland and the Free Churches in Wales and England provided the normal requirements of the law are met.

A Roman Catholic (of the Latin Rite – other rules apply for Oriental Rite Catholics) needs dispensation to marry someone who is not a Roman Catholic and a separate dispensation ('from canonical form') to marry outside the normal practice of the Roman Catholic Church. Thus the rite could be used where a Roman Catholic marries in another church provided the rules of the other Church allow this.

Canon 1120 of the Code of Canon Law (1983) states, 'The Bishops' Conference can draw up its own rite of marriage, to be reviewed by the Holy See, in keeping with the usages of the place and people, adapting these to the Christian spirit; however the law must be observed which requires that the person assisting at the marriage, being present, is to ask for and receive the expression of the contracting parties' consent.' This raises the possibility that the rite could be adopted by a national Conference of Catholic Bishops, with confirmation from Rome, as one of the Catholic rites for a particular Bishops' Conference.

The Marriage Act, 1949, describes marriages conducted in the Church of England as 'Marriages according to the Rites of the Church of England'. (The Act, by schedule, applies also to the Church in Wales, which Section 6 of the Welsh Church [Temporalities] Act, 1919, had exempted from the effects of disestablishment with respect to marriage.) Such marriages can only be solemnized by those whom the law recognizes as 'in Holy Orders'. Such marriages are solemnized under the authority of their respective churches and can therefore only be solemnized using forms of service authorized within their churches. The 1949 Act does not itself define what constitutes marriage 'according to the Rites of the Church of England'. It would appear that 'Marriage according to the Rites of the Church of England' refers to a marriage solemnized under the immediate authority of the Church of England or the Church in Wales.

The effect of this would appear to be that the JLG service could only be used in the Church of England or the Church in Wales if the Church in question authorizes it as a rite of that Church. Even without such explicit authorization, wherever the rubrics of an authorized rite of the Church so allow, elements of the JLG rite could be inserted in the service.

Canon B43.1(1)(e) of the Church of England provides that 'A minister or lay person who is a member of good standing of a Church to which this Canon applies and is a baptized person may, subject to the provisions of this Canon, be invited . . . to assist at . . . the Solemnization of Matrimony . . . if the minister or lay person is authorized to perform a similar duty in his or her own Church.' (The *Legal Opinions Concerning the Church of England* [1994, p173] give an interpretation of what sections of the service this may involve; these particular judgements may in time be modified by Notes governing a subsequent alternative marriage service. In another context the *Legal Opinions* [p171] identify the 'essential parts' of the rite as including 'the charge, promises and vows'.) The Church of England and the Church in Wales, like the Roman Catholic Church, require that a marriage be solemnized before an individual minister who must preside at the crucial moments of the rite. Working within this understanding, the JLG's service explicitly makes provision for a minister of another church to play a visible role at certain moments of the rite without compromising the presidency of the officiating minister.

The Marriage Act, 1949, provides

75. (I) Any person who knowingly and wilfully –

(b) solemnizes a marriage according to the rites of the Church of England without banns of matrimony having been duly published (not being a marriage solemnized on the authority of a special licence, a common licence or a certificate of a superintendent registrar);

(c) solemnizes a marriage according to the said rites (not being a marriage by special licence) in any place other than a church or other building in which banns may be published;

(d) solemnizes a marriage according to the said rites falsely pretending to be in Holy Orders;

shall be guilty of felony and shall be liable to imprisonment for a period not exceeding fourteen years.

The common understanding of this appears to be that a Free Church minister may use the words of an authorized marriage Anglican rite (where permitted by the rules of their own Church) provided he/she is not purporting to marry the couple 'according to the rites and ceremonies of the Church of England'. Thus the Registrar-General of Marriages does not routinely warn Free Church ministers in England and Wales against using the words of any authorized Anglican rite. However another view is that the Marriage Act, 1949, precludes any form of marriage service being used simultaneously by the Church of England (or the Church in Wales) and by a minister of the Free Churches in the same country. So, on this view, an Anglican minister could not preside at the JLG rite in non-Anglican places of worship if the rite has been authorized for use in an Anglican Church.

ACKNOWLEDGEMENTS

Affirmation by Families and Congregation, from *A Christian Celebration of Marriage: An Ecumenical Liturgy*, Fortress Press, 1987.

'Gracious God, as you have brought', from *The Methodist Service Book*.

The words introducing the exchange of consent, from the Roman Catholic Order of Christian Marriage.

'Bless, O God, the giving of these rings', from *A Christian Celebration of Marriage: An Ecumenical Liturgy*, Fortress Press, 1987.

'I give you this ring as a sign of our marriage', from *The Alternative Service Book 1980*, © The Central Board of Finance of the Church of England.

'My dear friends, let us ask God to pour out his blessing', from the Roman Catholic Order of Christian Marriage.

The second version is that of the English Language Liturgical Consultation in *Praying Together*, Canterbury Press, 1990.

'We have witnessed the wedding', from the Roman Catholic Order of Christian Marriage.

'My dear friends, let us ask God for his continued blessings', from the Roman Catholic Order of Christian Marriage.

'Father most holy...' Nuptial Blessing C from Segment Eight of *The Sacramentary*, © International Commission on English in the Liturgy.

'Let us pray. At the wedding in Cana...' adapted from an English translation of the Prayer of the Faithful in the Roman Catholic Irish Marriage Rite.

'Most gracious God', from *The Book of Common Prayer*, United States of America.

ADDRESS

Association of Interchurch Families, Inter-Church House, 35–41 Lower Marsh, London SE1 7RL.